Nigel Mansell

The Making of a Champion

Nigel Snowdon

(with additional material by Diana Burnett)

Aston Publications

Published in 1992 by
Aston Publications Limited
Bourne End House, Harvest Hill,
Bourne End, Bucks, SL8 5JJ

Designed by Alan Oliver

Printed and bound in Hong Kong

Sole distributor to the UK book trade
Springfield Books Limited
Norman Road, Denby Dale
Huddersfield
West Yorkshire, HD8 8TH

Sole distributor in the United States
Motorbooks International
729 Prospect Avenue, Osceola
Wisconsin 54020
United States

Nigel Mansell

The Making of a Champion

Contents

Now, in my thirtieth year of Grand Prix photography, I find the Formula 1 scene as enthralling as ever. The resurgence of the Williams team and the brilliance of Nigel Mansell revitalized racing and Nigel's chase of Championship leader Ayrton Senna throughout the latter part of the 1991 season swept away, perhaps for ever, the almost tedious McLaren domination of recent years. Then came what seemed to be complete Williams superiority in the early races of 1992. By winning five successive Grands Prix Mansell and Williams set a new Formula 1 record and it appeared that this superiority would in itself kill enthusiasm and interest in what is for me at least still the world's finest sport.

Then came Monaco, Nigel's tyre problems, a resurgence of McLaren strength and Senna's first win of the year. That the Championship was by no means 'cut and dried' became even more evident in Canada where the McLarens and Williams were closely matched, Nigel retired because of a rare mistake and Senna was eliminated by mechanical problems.

Nigel, at the time of writing, has an enormous lead in the Championship and he should win more races this year, but McLaren will have improved on a race-by-race basis and Senna will be fighting all the way. It has all the makings of proving one of the most exciting and memorable seasons in the history of Grand Prix racing.

I have been present at every Formula 1 race in which Nigel Mansell completed since his first rather uncertain debut at the Österreichring in 1980. In the paddock, in the pits, at testing sessions, parties, press conferences and launches and, above all, through the lens of my Nikon, I have seen Nigel develop into a great British Champion, one of the finest ever British drivers and one of the outstanding drivers of his generation. He is brave, immensely experienced, exceptionally quick, with superb judgement and reactions that seize and exploit the slightest opportunity. There is little more that any team could ask of its driver.

Nigel Mansell's break into Formula 1 was back in 1980 and he is now one of the longest-serving of all Grand Prix drivers. There was no instant success for Mansell and his early Formula 1 years with Lotus were largely frustrating and fruitless. His has been a career that has developed gradually, as he honed his skills, conserved his earnings and made wise financial investments. Moving first to the Isle of Man and latterly to Florida, he has created a contented lifestyle with Rosanne and children Leo (named after singer Leo Sayer), Chloe and Greg (named after his close friend golfer Greg Norman). Whether or not Nigel has won the 1992 Drivers' Championship, his retirement from racing is not likely to be long delayed.

Nigel Snowdon
Maidstone
May 1992

The young Nigel Mansell.

1   THE EARLY YEARS

When Nigel Mansell entered Formula Ford 1600 with his own Hawke DL11 in 1976, he was already vastly experienced in another field of motor sport. Born at Upton-on-Severn on 9 August, 1954, Nigel's family were motor racing enthusiasts and his father Eric had competed in Karting. That he should be encouraged to do the same is not surprising. He competed regularly in Kart racing, soon appearing in international events.

With the Hawke, Nigel, supported as always by wife Rosanne, competed in only 11 races, but he won five and set fastest lap in five. For 1977 Nigel was rewarded for his solo efforts with drives in Formula Ford 1600 in a Javelin JL5 entered by Patrick Mulleady. Although the Javelin was not the most competitive of Formula Ford cars, Nigel succeded in taking several second and third places and also won a heat at Silverstone. By May of 1977 Nigel had realized that he had no future with the Javelin, arranged to borrow a more competitive Crossle 25F and ran in the name of well-known entrant Alan McKechnie. He drove the 25F in six races, of which he won three and McKechnie then entered him at the wheel of the latest Crossle 32F provided by an impressed John Crossle. With the new car Mansell won 11 races and finals and took the Brush Fusegear Championship. McKechnie also entered him in a small number of Formula 3 races with Puma and Lola cars, but they were uncompetitive and his best result was a fourth place at Silverstone in October.

There was no sponsorship for 1978 and so Nigel and Rosanne made a difficult, some would say dangerous, decision. The decision was reached to sell their house in Hall Green, Birmingham (and buy a smaller property) and to sell some family paintings. The proceeds were 'invested' in a works March Formula 3 drive. Nigel gave up his job with Girling-Lucas as a hydro-mechanical engineer to concentrate on racing, while Rosanne supplemented the family income with a job at the Gas Board. Nigel's season with March lasted only five races before the money ran out, but on his first outing he took pole position at the International Trophy meeting at Silverstone and finished second to Nelson Piquet.

Nigel's last drive at Donington Park in April won him a drive in a Formula 2 race with the ICI Chevron team at Donington Park in June, but it was to prove a great disappointment. He crashed in pre-race testing on the Tuesday before the race and in official practice the Chevron was slow through the corners, plagued by tyre problems and lacked balance. Mansell's mechanic was absent so the car could not be set up properly and the spare was given to Elio de Angelis. It is hardly surprising that he failed to qualify.

Nigel Mansell ' s racing career started in 1976 when he entered his own Hawke DL11 in Formula Ford 1600. He ran in eleven races, won five and set fastest lap in five. Here, No. 50, Nigel is seen at Mallory Park in September 1976 when he took second place.

In 1977 Nigel drove a full season in Formula Ford 1600, initially with a Javelin JL5 entered by Patrick Mulleady and later with Crossle 25F and 32F cars entered by Alan McKechnie. Nigel is seen with the Javelin at Silverstone.

Mansell did not lack supporters and strong canvassing, some of it from March, resulted in a regular drive in 1979 with the Unipart-sponsored March-Triumph Formula 3 team. The Unipart cars were no match for the more usual Toyota-powered versions and Nigel struggled all year. He competed in 19 races, and his best results were a win at Silverstone in March (but only after Andrea de Cesaris had been penalized for missing the chicane), together with two second places.

His season was marred by a bad crash at Oulton Park in September. Nigel was chasing the leader, Eddie Jordan, when de Cesaris aimed for a gap that simply wasn't there and T-boned Mansell's March which flipped over heavily on to the roll-over bar. Nigel suffered severe bruising to the lower back and broken vertebrae in the neck. The magazine *Autosport* contacted Nigel at Chester Hospital on the Monday and he was fit enough to comment, '... I looked in my mirrors coming down the hill and saw that de Cesaris was a little closer, but I was right behind Eddie Jordan [the leader] and I never thought he would try to come past. And the next thing I knew I was rolling over. I couldn't believe it.' Nigel went on to thank everyone who had helped after the accident, 'Especially the chap who held the drip on the way to the hospital ...'

Nigel returned to the works March team in 1980 with some financial backing from Pace Petroleum (at that time a full Formula 3 season cost about £60,000). By the end of May Nigel's season with the team was over and after nine races he had scored three fourths, a fifth and two sixths. Mansell had concluded that the latest March 803 was a thoroughly bad car and those who were involved with the team at the time still argue whether Nigel left March or was pushed. A week after his last drive with March Nigel appeared at the wheel of one of former Brabham boss Ron Tauranac's works Formula 2 cars at Silverstone. Nigel's only success with the Honda-powered Ralt was a second place at Hockenheim in September. By this time Mansell had driven for Lotus at three Formula 1 races and a new chapter in his career was opening.

Mansell also drove for Alan McKechnie three times in Formula 3 in 1977 and he is seen here in his third drive in the 'Gone in 60 seconds' race at Thruxton in November. Nigel's Lola T570-Toyota was handicapped by a lack of straight-line speed and he finished fifth.

Nigel with the Alan McKechnie-entered Crossle 32F at Donington Park in July 1977. Because of broken vertebrae in the neck suffered in a crash at Brands Hatch the previous weekend, he drove with a special neck brace; he won both his heat and the final and set fastest lap in both.

Lack of finance meant that Nigel appeared at only five Formula 3 races in 1978, but he was also given a Formula 2 drive with the ICI Chevron-Hart team in June. He is seen during pre-race testing when he went off on oil dropped by another car and damaged the monocoque. Mainly because of tyre problems and lack of speed through the corners he failed to qualify.

For 1979 Nigel gained a regular drive with the Unipart team which fielded Triumph-powered March 783 Formula 3 cars. Here, in September, Mansell leads a string of cars at Thruxton. He finished eighth. The Unipart team struggled all season and Nigel won only one race, after the leader on the road had been penalized.

Nigel Mansell in 1980.

Nigel Mansell with the Formula 2 Ralt in the pits at Silverstone in 1980.

Nigel Mansell at the wheel of the Formula 2 Ralt at Silverstone in 1980.

Nigel Mansell with the Formula 2 Honda-powered Ralt RH6 at Silverstone 1980.

2 *LEARNING CURVE AT LOTUS, 1980-84*

1979

In September Nigel was invited to take part in a Team Lotus testing session at the Paul Ricard circuit in the South of France. The others taking part were Elio de Angelis, already in Formula 1 with the Shadow team, Eddie Cheever (who entered Formula 1 in 1980 with Osella and later drove for Renault), Jan Lammers (who drove an Ensign in 1980) and very successful Formula 2 driver Stephen South whose career was brought short by a bad accident.

At this time the Lotus team was in very real difficulties. Mario Andretti had won the World Championship in 1978 with the ground-effect 79, but the 1979 80 car had proved too complex, for most of the year the team had relied on the 1978 cars and it failed to win a single race. Drivers Mario Andretti and Carlos Reutemann were restless, Reutemann left at the end of the year to join Williams and Lotus lost its Martini sponsorship.

For the second time in his short career Nigel was suffering from broken vertebrae in the neck, the result of an accident at Oulton Park a few days previously. He knew that the testing session was too important to miss and, despite relying on painkillers, his driving greatly impressed Chapman.

De Angelis secured the number two seat in the Formula 1 team and Nigel was awarded a testing contract. The prospects of this leading to a regular Formula 1 seat were slim, but it was an important step in any driver's career.

1980

During 1980 Nigel combined testing the Lotus 81, that year's largely unsuccessful Formula 1 car, covering more than a thousand miles, with drives in Formula 3 and 2. By the middle of the year Chapman was thinking forward to 1981. It was known that Andretti would be leaving the team (he joined Alfa Romeo) and Chapman decided to enter a third 81, the longer-wheelbase 81B, in the Austrian Grand Prix for Mansell. Grand Prix racing was at the height of its ground-effect folly. With rock-hard suspension and sliding skirts that glued the cars to the track, the drivers were brutally pounded and the cars were difficult to control. At the fast, demanding Österreichring with lap speeds of 140 mph - and on which he had not driven previously - his 81 was plagued in practice by mechanical problems and it seemed unlikely that he would qualify. As the second practice session was nearing the end, Chapman ordered a swap of cars with de Angelis and Nigel snatched last place on the grid. Just before the start of the race the fuel was topped up on the start line, but some was carelessly sloshed into the cockpit and within a few laps had seeped through his overalls, causing him acute pain and first degree burns. Engine failure after 40 laps brought an end to his misery.

Nigel Mansell's first Formula 1 drive with the Essex Lotus team came at the 1980 Austrian Grand Prix.

In Austria Mansell scraped on to the back of the grid, but he was soaked by fuel just before the start and he drove in extreme pain until the engine failed.

Mansell reappeared with the 81B at the Dutch Grand Prix at Zandvoort. He qualified comfortably with the team's spare 81 car, but had to drive the ill-handling 81B in the race. It was to prove a short race. On lap 16 the brakes failed and Nigel spun the 81 for 100 yards until the skirts brought it to a rest on the grass verge. Nigel was entered again at the Italian Grand Prix, but became a non-qualifier after he spun off, lightly touching the crash barriers, and the abandoned Lotus was rammed by Winkelhock's Arrows. Apart from a Formula 2 race at Hockenheim a fortnight later, he never again drove in a lesser formula.

1981

For 1981 Mansell was offered a regular place in the Lotus team. He was ambitious, hungry for success and immensely fit after a sustained weight training programme at his home at Hall Green in Birmingham. But it was not to be an easy year. Team Lotus was in its second year of sponsorship from Essex, the oil company headed by that shadowy figure, David Thieme.

Following the ban on sliding skirts for the 1981 season, Colin Chapman had devised a twin-chassis design to circumvent the ban. The 'primary' chassis consisted of the monocoque and conventional suspension while there was also a secondary chassis constructed in moulded carbon-composite, supported by its own framework and carrying the bodywork, side-pods, wings and radiators. While the driver had a comparatively softly suspended ride in the primary structure, the secondary structure, insulated from the driver, transmitted the aerodynamic loads directly to the tyre contact areas. Both Mansell and de Angelis extensively tested the prototype 86, and for the 1981 season the definitive twin-chassis car was the 88. Chapman also developed the conventional 87, in case the 88 should face legality problems.

The season started with the non-Championship South African Grand Prix, non-Championship because sliding skirts were still permitted, but Mansell was a poor tenth, although his team-mate de Angelis finished third. Although Lotus entered the 88s at the first round of the Championship at Long Beach, Chapman knew that the team would face difficulties. De Angelis drove one of the new cars in the first practice session, the cars were disqualified and the practice time disallowed. Lotus reverted to the old 81s. On appeal, the car was recognised as legal, but it was immediately made clear by FISA that this decision applied in the United States only.

Chapman tried again at the Brazilian Grand Prix, another fraught race for the team. When Lotus team manager Peter Collins found himself in difficulties in a strong current whilst swimming from the beach in front of the team's hotel, it was Mansell who struck out and rescued the Australian. Whilst Collins - and de Angelis who had also found himself in difficulties - were completely exhausted after this dangerous incident, Mansell, immensely fit thanks to his weight-training programme, was still breathing normally as if he had undergone no abnormal exertion. Back at Rio Autodromo the 88s were again disqualified and the 81s substituted.

Mansell's second Formula 1 race was the 1980 Dutch Grand Prix. In the pits at Zandvoort Nigel talks to team manager Peter Collins. His race engineer Nigel Stroud is with Colin Chapman who is watching lap times. Team sponsor David Thieme in the stetson.

In the 1980 Dutch Grand Prix.

In the 1981 non-Championship South African Grand Prix Nigel finished a poor tenth.

Mansell with the Lotus 81 leads Jean-Pierre Jarier (Talbot-Ligier) in the 1981 United States Grand Prix West at Long Beach. Mansell slid off into a wall, possibly the result of damage caused during an accident in the untimed morning session.

The Lotus 88s were disqualified again in the Argentine, the third race in succession and later that month finally banned by an FIA International Court of Appeal in Paris. That same month sponsor David Thieme was arrested in Zurich. The team and drivers were in a state of near-despair and Lotus withdrew from the San Marino Grand Prix. But there was still fight left in the team and in Belgium Nigel drove an 81 into a gritty and determined third place after a long battle with Gilles Villeneuve's turbocharged Ferrari. He followed this up with third place on the grid at Monaco at the wheel of the 87 and held third place in the race until a rear suspension link broke. Two magnificent performances and Nigel's reputation was growing.

But the 87 was uncompetitive, no match for the Brabham and Williams opposition and every race was a struggle. Chapman was still determined to race the twin-chassis 88. In June he showed the Royal Automobile Club a slightly revised version and the RAC Technical Commission indicated that it regarded the new 88B as legal. Both Mansell and de Angelis practised with the 88Bs on the Thursday morning at the Grand Prix meeting, but FISA intervened, the RAC was forced to accept their decision that the cars were illegal and they were again disqualified. An 87 was brought from the Lotus works at Hethel for de Angelis and the team hastily converted an 88B to 87 specification for Mansell to drive in Friday's practice. The burden was too great and whilst de Angelis scraped into the race, near the back of the grid, Nigel failed to qualify.

For the remainder of the year the uphill struggle continued and little success came the way of Team Lotus. Mansell rounded off the season with a fourth place in the Caesars Palace Grand Prix at Las Vegas, had gained eight points in the World Championship and finished the season with a much enhanced reputation.

1982

There was a steadily growing bond between Nigel Mansell and Colin Chapman and the British driver was happy to stay with Team Lotus for another season. Chapman had put the twin-chassis concept behind him and under the direction of Peter Wright the team had produced a new car, the 91. Sadly, it was to be a year of frustration and failure and the 91 was to prove an also-ran. Increasingly, Mansell's talents, but not his determination, were being masked by the inadequacies of his cars.

In the early part of the year Nigel's only 'success' was third place in the Brazilian Grand Prix, but this was because of the disqualification of Nelson Piquet and Keke Rosberg who had finished first and second on the road. As part of a continuing war between FISA and the Formula One Constructors' Association, Lotus, together with all the other British teams except Tyrrell, withdrew from the San Marino Grand Prix. The Canadian race brought more problems for Nigel. On the second lap Bruno Giacomelli slowed suddenly as he headed for the pits; Mansell, following the Alfa Romeo closely, locked his brakes and the Lotus rode over the tail of the Italian car. Nigel's left hand slipped off the spinning steering wheel which trapped his left arm. His forearm was badly sprained and he was forced to miss the Dutch Grand Prix. He returned at the British Grand Prix, his left arm fitted with a special cast, and not really fit enought to drive. In immense pain he qualified 23rd out of 26 starters, but the pain forced him to retire after 30 laps.

During the remainder of this miserable year he failed to finish in the first six and his total score in the World Championship was a mere 7 points.

At the wheel of the uncompetitive Lotus 81 after the controversial 'twin-chassis' 88 had been disqualified at the second race in succession in Brazil.

Waiting to practice with the 81 in Brazil.

Lotus supporters at the Belgian race at Zolder demand the twin-chassis 88

Nigel proved his ability at Zolder by taking third place with the 81 behind Carlos Reutemann (Williams) and Jacques Laffite (Talbot-Ligier).

The last race in full Essex colours. Mansell took third place on the grid at Monaco with the new 87 and ran a fine third until a rear suspension link broke.

By the Spanish race Team Lotus was again resplendent in John Player Special black and gold colours, with Essex a subsidiary sponsor. Mansell enhanced his rapidly-growing reputation with a hard-fought sixth place.

With the 87 at the French Grand Prix at Dijon-Prenois, Mansell finished seventh.

Nigel Mansell in his Lotus 87 during the second practice session at the 1981 British Grand Prix; he failed to qualify.

Prior to the 1981 British Grand Prix the Lotus team tested extensively with the modified 88B twin-chassis cars, as well as the 87. Mansell waits with the 87 while adjustments are made to the rear wing. The 88B is in the front of the garage.

1983

For 1983 Team Lotus had entered into an arrangement with Renault for the supply of turbocharged engines. It was known however that initially only sufficient Renault engines would be available for one car, to be driven by de Angelis, while Mansell was to drive a new Cosworth-powered car, the 92, but with 'Active' computer-controlled suspension. It was during the early testing of the 92, on 16 December 1982, that Colin Chapman suffered a heart attack and died. Chapman's death was a terrible blow to Mansell, for he and Chapman had developed a close relationship, something that often happened between the Lotus boss and his drivers and it was not to be repeated with other teams that Mansell drove for in later years. In 1982 Peter Warr had returned to manage Team Lotus, relationships between Warr and Mansell were far from easy and steadily deteriorated. Nigel resented Warr's decision that Elio de Angelis should drive the turbocharged car, because of his better results, while Warr considered that Mansell had assumed the airs and graces of a 'superstar'.

Both cars proved dreadful, ill-handling, lacking in reliability and uncompetitive. Lotus had only too obviously lost its sense of direction. At one event, the Race of Champions, Mansell drove the turbocharged 93T, but retired because of handling problems. The 92 was almost as bad, even when the 'Active' suspension had been abandoned after Long Beach. After finishing 12th in the first two Championship races, Brazil and Long Beach, Nigel retired from the French Grand Prix in unusual circumstances. Before the race he had been talking to crew chief Bob Dance in the pits, the noise of engines drowned a warning shout as the mechanics rolled the spare car on heavy setting-up wheels into the garage. One of the wheels rolled over Nigel's left foot and he suffered injured toes. Such was the pain that he retired after only six laps. At Imola Mansell retired when the rear wing broke off at close to 170 mph and at Monaco he was eliminated in a first-lap collision with Alboreto's Tyrrell. A sixth place followed at Detroit and he retired again at Montreal.

After the Belgian race Team Lotus was joined by the vastly experienced Gérard Ducarouge whose brief was to design a new car powered by the Renault engine as speedily as possible. The result was the 94T, based on the 1982 type 91 monocoque. The 94T was a vast improvement on its predecessor and in his first race with the new car, the British Grand Prix, Mansell drove a stirring race and finished fourth. Later he took a fifth place in Austria and, in the European Grand Prix at Brands Hatch, turned in his best performance of the season, third place.

At the Austrian Grand Prix in 1981, Nigel Mansell talks to Nigel Stroud.

In the rain-soaked 1981 Canadian Grand Prix. Nigel was eliminated in a collision with Alan Prost (Renault).

Lotus raced the new, very simple, but attractive 91 in 1982. Nigel is seen in the United States Grand Prix West at Long Beach where he finished seventh, two places behind team-mate Elio de Angelis.

1984

By 1984 Lotus - and Peter Warr in particular - wanted to replace Mansell and he would have liked to have escaped the strained atmosphere of the team. Sponsors John Player were however anxious to retain his services and Nigel decided, with some reluctance, to stay for another season. The 1984 car was the 95T, still with the Renault engine, but with a completely new carbon/Kevlar monocoque. Despite all Nigel's efforts, it was to prove another disappointing year. After retiring in the first four races, he took a fine third place in France behind Lauda (McLaren) and Tambay (Renault), pushing to the back of his mind his grief at the death of his mother a few days previously.

Then came Monaco where Mansell was second fastest in practice. The race was held in torrential rain and Mansell drove magnificently, coming through to take the lead from Alain Prost on lap 11 - the first time in his career that he had led a Grand Prix - and he gradually extended his lead. As Alan Henry commented in *Autocourse* 'Frankly the Englishman was running too quickly when he didn't have to do so.' Six laps after he took the lead, on the long climb from Ste. Devote to Casino Square he lost control on the white line painted down the road and slammed into the guard-rail. With deflated rear tyre and damaged aerofoil he carried on to Mirabeau corner where he spun out of the race. All that was left to him was to sit on the guard-rail with his head in his hands. It was a failure that he found difficult to accept. To Mansell it seemed unreasonable that such a small error should have thrown away the race, whereas it is not making mistakes that wins races.

As a result of the Monaco accident Mansell began to try too hard. In Canada he finished sixth, after falling back from fourth place because of gearbox trouble and after the race he and team-mate de Angelis fell out badly - Nigel was angry with the Italian who had blocked him for lap after lap. At Detroit he made a near perfect start from the second row, but collided with Piquet's Brabham and because of other accidents on that first lap the race was stopped. Mansell was fined $6000 for dangerous driving and there was talk of suspending his licence. In the restarted race he retired because of gearbox trouble.

More problems followed at Dallas where Nigel took the first pole position in his career, and led for the first 35 laps on this difficult, bumpy circuit. Under pressure from Rosberg (Honda), he scraped a wall, Rosberg went ahead and Mansell hit the wall again, damaging the gearbox. He tried to push the car to the line, but became unconscious in the intense heat. De Angelis finished third and Rosberg scathingly criticized Mansell for holding him up for so many laps.

A fourth place followed in Germany, but soon afterwards Lotus announced that Ayrton Senna would be joining the team for 1985. It was unsaid, but obvious that Mansell would be leaving. Mansell fought on doggedly, finishing third in Holland, but retiring in the other four races that completed the season. Nigel could so easily have slipped into obscurity at the end of 1984, but secured a drive alongside Rosberg in the Williams team. It was to prove the start of a new era.

At Monaco Nigel drove the 91 to a fine fourth place beating team-mate Elio de Angelis.

With race engineer Steve Hallam at Monaco in 1982.

Nigel Mansell with the Lotus 91 in the 82 British Grand Prix. He retired because of handling problems.

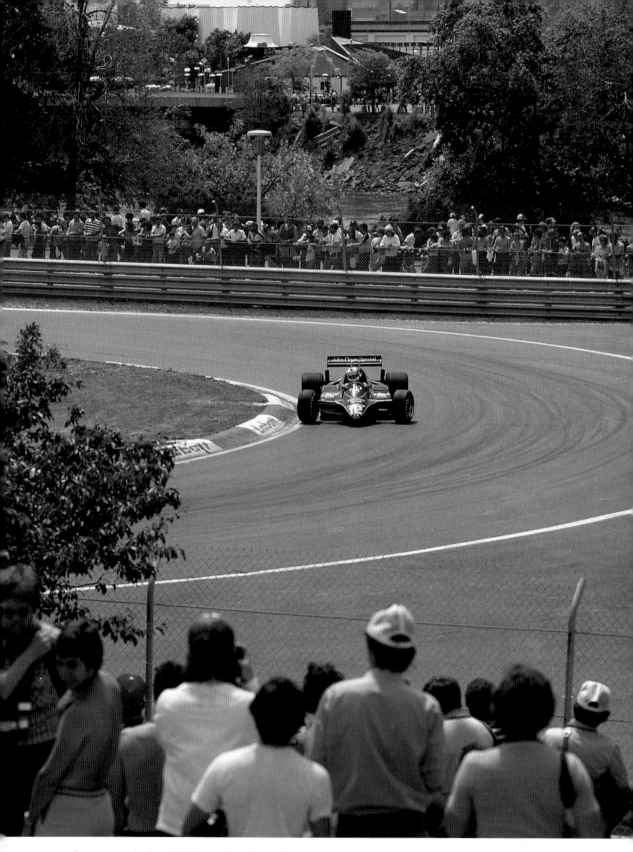

In practice for the 1982 Canadian Grand Prix on the scenic Circuit Gilles Villeneuve at Montreal. Mansell was eliminated on the second lap when he rode over the rear of Giacomelli's Alfa Romeo. The Italian driver had without warning slowed to return to the pits. Because of a sprained forearm Nigel missed the Dutch race.

After losing to the author at backgammon in Rio de Janeiro, Nigel Mansell dumped Snowdon into a laundry basket and propelled it into the hotel swimming pool.

In the 1983 Brazilian Grand Prix, Elio de Angelis leads Nigel Mansell. Mansell finished a poor 12th, while de Angelis was disqualified because he had switched from the Renault-powered 93T to a Cosworth-powered 92 after the warm-up lap.

In practice at Monaco with the 92, the last Cosworth-powered Lotus. Mansell was eliminated on the first lap by a collision with Alboreto's Tyrrell.

At the British Grand Prix the Lotus team had introduced the much improved 94T. Nigel is in the Austrian race in which he finished fifth.

Relaxing at the Austrian Grand Prix.

In the 1983 Dutch Grand Prix at Zandvoort. Mansell spun off after passing Derek Warwick's Toleman, the sort of error of judgement that he stopped making a long time ago.

With the turbocharged Lotus 95T in the 1984 French Grand Prix in which he took third place.

At Monaco in 1984 Mansell was second fastest in practice and in the torrentially wet race took the lead from Prost (McLaren). It was a short-lived lead, however, for after another five laps he slid into the barriers on the climb to the Casino. It was the greatest disappointment in his career.

Waiting to practise at the 1984 British Grand Prix at Brands Hatch.

3 CHAMPIONSHIP CHALLENGE, WILLIAMS, 1985-88

1985

The Williams team, headed by Frank Williams, had been running cars with turbocharged Honda engines since late 1983 and the 1985 FW10 was their first car with a carbon-composite monocoque. The power band of the Honda engine was at this time acutely narrow and great skill was needed to exploit the potential of the Japanese V6 engine. Initially Finnish driver Keke Rosberg, who had been with Williams for some years and had won the 1982 Drivers' Championship with a Cosworth-powered Williams, had not been at all well disposed towards Mansell joining the team, but the two drivers soon came to work amicably together. Although Nigel was to make a bad start to the year, the combination of working in a team with a friendly and encouraging approach to racing and the improvements made to the cars during the year by designer Patrick Head were to lead to a good measure of success.

Mansell started the year badly in Brazil. At the green light he accelerated with the Williams through from the third row of the grid, tried to pass Alboreto (Ferrari) for second place at the first corner, the two cars collided, the Williams rose in the air and spun on to the grass. Alboreto continued but Mansell was out of the race. Although Nigel denied it strongly, most onlookers – and Alboreto – believed the British driver to be at fault. Fifth places followed in Portugal and at Imola, he was seventh because of brake trouble at Monaco and sixth in Canada. Brake trouble caught Mansell out at Detroit where he hit a concrete wall, was briefly concussed and suffered a badly jarred right thumb.

The season was proving a repetition of previous misfortunes and continued in practice in France. Travelling at a good 200 mph he lost control when the left rear Goodyear failed, strands of rubber flailed through the suspension on that side of the Williams, and the car hit a concrete post which tore off the left front suspension and his helmet was hit by the wheel. He was badly concussed and unable to start the race. Mansell bounced back to appear in the British race at Silverstone, but retired because of clutch failure.

It was only now that Mansell's year began to take off. After sixth places in Germany and Holland and engine failure in Austria and at Monza where he set fastest lap, the British racing hero's star really shone. In practice for the Belgian race he had another frightening moment when the steering wheel broke on one of Spa's fast downhill sweeps, but his race performance was unaffected and after a spin and two off-course excursions he finished second to Senna (Lotus).

At Brands Hatch, scene of the European Grand Prix, Nigel finally achieved the win that he had so long awaited. After a superb start from the second row of the grid, he tried to run round the outside of Senna at Paddock Bend, Senna held his line and Mansell was forced on to the dirt, resuming in fourth place. Rosberg spun off while trying to pass Senna, Piquet's Brabham collided with the Williams and while the Finn limped back to the pits to change a punctured tyre, Piquet was out of the race with bent suspension. Nigel was now

With the Williams FW10 in Brazil in 1985, Mansell collided with Alboreto's Ferrari at the first corner and retired a few laps later.

Nigel crashed at close to 200 mph in practice for the 1985 French Grand Prix at the Paul Ricard circuit, the result of tyre failure, and failed to start the race.

At the 1985 British Grand Prix.

After winning the 1985 European Grand Prix at Brands Hatch.

in second place, chasing Senna hard. When Rosberg rejoined the race, he came out of the pits just in front of the leaders. Through Druids and Bottom Bend Rosberg held up Senna enough to give Nigel his chance and he sneaked through into the lead. All this had happened in the first nine laps of the race and Nigel stayed in front for the remaining 66. This first Grand Prix win justified for Nigel - and Rosanne - all the years of fruitless effort. It was a turning point in his career and his driving became more confident, more assured and more mature.

A second victory followed in Canada where Nigel took pole position. He led from the start, was passed by Rosberg on lap 9, but the Finn almost immediately spun on oil dropped by Ghinzani's Toleman and Nigel went ahead again. At the finish he was just under 8 seconds ahead of his team-mate.

In Australia Nigel fell victim on the first lap to a charging Senna and Rosberg was the winner. Nigel finished sixth in the Drivers' Championship with 31 points.

1986

Keke Rosberg left to drive for McLaren and Nigel was joined in the team by Brazilian Nelson Piquet. Piquet, an adversary from Formula 3 days, had already won two Drivers' Championships for Brabham. Williams possessed the most formidable team in Formula 1, but relations between Mansell and Rosberg were strained and difficult as both struggled for supremacy in the Drivers' Championship. In March Frank Williams was seriously injured in a car crash while returning from testing at the Paul Ricard circuit. Williams was absent from the circuits for much of the year - and when he did recover he was confined to a wheelchair - but so good was the Didcot team's organization that the team's success was unaffected by his absence. The latest Williams was the FW11, still Honda-powered, but extensively modified.

Nigel started the season badly in Brazil where he was dashed into the barriers by Senna yet again at the first corner. With Mansell out of the race Piquet was able to score an easy win. Next came the Spanish race at Estoril. After a late stop for tyres Nigel pulled back almost 20 seconds on Senna to be beaten by a mere 1.1 seconds at the chequered flag. So close was the finish that Nigel initially believed that he had won.

After retiring because of engine trouble at Imola, Nigel finished fourth at Monaco with a car that seemed down on power. On the beautiful and difficult Spa-Francorchamps circuit, scene of the Belgian Grand Prix, Nigel made a superbly judged stop for new tyres, the Williams team were slicker than the Lotus and Mansell was able to move up into second place ahead of Senna, taking the lead when Johansson pitted his Ferrari. At the finish Nigel was almost 40 seconds ahead of Senna who had settled for a safe second place. In Canada Nigel's record of wins became four and in another superbly judged race he led almost throughout. He was now in second place in the Championship with 27 points to the 29 of Prost.

Plagued by brake trouble Nigel was a poor fifth at Detroit. A fourth victory followed in France. Patrick Head had determined on two stops for tyres, calculating that the time lost would be outweighed by the advantages of the fresh rubber. Mansell dominated the race and won by over 20 seconds from Prost (McLaren). There was more than an element of luck in Nigel's next victory in the British Grand Prix.

At Monaco in 1986 where he finished fourth
with the Honda-powered Williams FW11.

The marshals applaud Mansell at the finish of the 1986 Monaco Grand Prix in which he finished fourth.

Telling all to BBC commentator Murray Walker at the 1986 French Grand Prix.

At the British Grand Prix at Brands Hatch the Williams team scored a magnificent 1-2, Mansell leading Piquet across the line.

Immediately after the start Nigel's Williams was out because of a broken drive-shaft, but the race was stopped because of a multi-car accident and Mansell was able to join the restart. After a race-long battle Mansell won by just over 5 seconds from his team-mate to be mobbed by his supporters. Nigel now led the Championship with 47 points to the 43 of Prost. Third place followed in Germany where Nigel struggled with handling problems. The winner was Piquet and Piquet won again in Hungary while Nigel was again third, convinced that Piquet's car had some technical advantage.

Both Williams drivers retired in Austria, Piquet won at Monza with Nigel second and Nigel won in Portugal with Piquet third. Relationships between the two drivers deteriorated further as Nigel accused Piquet of misleading him about the advantages of a new differential and rear wing that the Brazilian had tried. Nelson merely shrugged his shoulders ... In Mexico Williams expected to dominate and Mansell was hoping to clinch the World Championship. Troubled by a stomach upset Nigel fumbled the start and began a long chase of Piquet. The Brazilian finished fourth after tyre problems, but kept the door firmly shut on Mansell who finished an unhappy fifth.

All now rested on the Australian Grand Prix. Nigel still led the Championship with a net 70 points to the 64 of Alain Prost and 63 of Nelson Piquet. Only the 11 best results from the 16 rounds counted and if either Prost or Piquet won at Adelaide, Mansell had to finish no worse than third. After Monaco Nigel had returned home to the Isle of Man to get as much rest as possible before this vital encounter. He arrived at the circuit determined to go all out for a win rather than drive a tactical race to gain the minimum number of points necessary.

Nigel started from pole position, but was passed by Senna, Piquet and Rosberg. Senna retired after 43 laps and Mansell's third place was good enough for him not to worry. Rosberg retired and Piquet and Mansell held first and second places. On lap 64 Mansell was coming up to lap Alliot's Ligier when the left rear tyre exploded at close to 180 mph in sixth gear. Tyre debris flew in all directions, sparks showered from the left rear suspension and as this sank, so the right front wheel lifted clear of the road. Nigel battled with the wheel, forcing the Williams up the escape road and coming to rest with a gentle bump against the wall. With the Championship lost, his hopes dashed, his laconic comment was, 'I'm just happy to be alive' as he returned to the pits.

Piquet was called in for a precautionary tyre change and finished second behind Prost. The Frenchman took the World Championship with 72 points to the 70 of Mansell and 69 of Nelson Piquet.

In the Australian Grand Prix Nigel was in third place and seemed set to win his first World Championship. Then, at 180 mph, the left rear Goodyear exploded. As the left rear sank, so the right front wheel lifted. Mansell slid down the straight, fighting for control, and on down the escape road. It was the bitterest blow in his career.

On his way to a win in the 1987 San Marino Grand Prix at Imola, ahead of Ayrton Senna's Lotus.

Throughout 1987 bitter rivalry characterized the relationship between Mansell and Nelson Piquet as they struggled for supremacy in the World Championship. In the French race, which he won, Nigel maintained a narrow lead over Piquet who finished second.

1987

Nigel spent an introspective winter in the Isle of Man and it took several weeks for him to overcome this crushing defeat by fate. He bounced back into 1987 with a different sense of priorities, but with relations between himself and Piquet confined to a passing nod. The 1987 Williams FW11B was to prove the dominant car and the team was to dominate the World Championship. Mansell was to take pole position eight times and win six races, but again the Championship was to elude him.

The Williams team was plagued by overheating problems in Brazil where Prost won from Piquet and Mansell was a poor sixth despite taking pole position. The first of Nigel's six wins came at Imola, but both drivers retired in Belgium. At Spa Mansell and Senna had collided on the first lap; the Brazilian was out of the race, in the sand-trap, but Nigel continued for another 17 laps before coming into the pits. He went straight to the Lotus pit and straight for Senna - a confrontation that was only stopped when three mechanics dragged Mansell away. The rights and wrongs of the actual incident were overshadowed by the bad newspaper publicity.

Another retirement followed at Monaco where Piquet was second, Piquet and Mansell finished second and fifth at Detroit, but then at last Nigel's year started to come right. He won both the French and British races, trouncing Piquet. Piquet won in Germany after Prost retired shortly before the finish. Mansell dominated in Hungary until the right rear wheel shed its retaining nut and, as so often happened in 1987, Piquet was positioned to take the lead and win the race. Mansell won in Austria with Piquet second. At Monza Honda announced that they would be parting company with Williams, a savage decision that was totally unjustified at a time when the team was producing superb results. Piquet and Mansell took first two places on the grid at Monza and Piquet won with Mansell, slowed by rising water temperature and an engine power loss, a disappointed third. Nigel was an early retirement in Portugal, he scored a fine win in Spain and Piquet now led the Championship with 70 points to the 52 of Mansell and 51 of Senna. Nigel won again at Mexico City with Piquet second and had closed the gap with 61 points to the 73 of Piquet. There were two races to go and Nigel was still in with a chance.

Then came the Japanese Grand Prix at Suzuka. During the first qualifying session Nigel lost control of the Williams at high speed and careered backwards into a tyre barrier. It was not an accident caused by over-exuberance or trying too hard, but the very real risk faced by a topline driver at the knife-edge limit of his and the car's abilities. Mansell suffered severe bruising and muscle strain and was badly shocked. The medical advice was firm: not only could he not drive at Suzuka, but he would have to miss the Australian race. Piquet retired in Japan and Australia, but still took his third World Championship with Nigel in second place. It seemed that the British driver's chance would never come.

At the Paul Ricard circuit Nigel discusses practice with team boss Frank Williams.

'Go Nige Go' - the 1987 British Grand Prix

And Nige obliged. He takes the chequered flag to win the
British race with Piquet just under two seconds behind.

But it was not to be a Mansell Championship. In the 1987 German race he pulled off because of a seized engine.

Although Mansell later won the Austrian, Spanish and Mexican Grands Prix, Piquet won the Championship by eight points after Mansell crashed heavily in practice for the Japanese race.
In Austria Mansell leads Gerhard Berger (Ferrari) and Teo Fabi (Benetton).

1988

The 1988 season was the last when turbocharged engines were permitted, but some teams were already using the 3500cc normally aspirated engines that were to become mandatory in 1989 . Following the loss of Honda power, Williams opted for the V8 3500cc Judd. Piquet had left to drive for Lotus and Nigel was joined in the team by vastly experienced Italian driver Riccardo Patrese. That the Williams cars would prove uncompetitive seemed inevitable and team relations deteriorated badly. Much of this was blamed on Nigel who was said to have assumed 'superstar status'. But the sad truth was that he was a superstar without a competitive car. What little success he achieved in 1988 was by determined, superbly judged driving.

Following the Suzuka accident Nigel did not reappear at the wheel of a Formula 1 car until the testing at the Spanish Jerez circuit early in the year. Much of 1988 was a complete disaster as retirement followed retirement. In 14 of the year's 16 races that he competed in, Nigel finished only twice, in the British and Spanish races. By the Silverstone race the Williams FW12 was a much improved car and in a race held in intermittent rain he drove brilliantly to set fastest lap and finish 26 seconds behind winner Ayrton Senna. Something had to give and it was at this race that he announced that he would be joining Ferrari in 1989. Soon afterwards he contracted a secondary chicken-pox infection from daughter Chloe, but despite medical advice that he should miss the race, he turned up at the Hungarian Grand Prix unshaven and fraught. After 40 laps his vision started to blur and he eventually pulled into the pits to retire.

Nigel's place at Spa was taken by Martin Brundle and at Monza by Jean-Louis Schlesser. He returned to racing at the Portuguese race and turned in another stirring drive pursuing Senna's McLaren until he clipped the back of the McLaren and hit the guard-rail. A brilliant second place followed in Spain where he had pressured winner Prost in the early laps of the race, but dropped back because of a slow pit stop for new tyres.

It had been a disappointing, frustrating year, but Nigel knew that he fortunes could only improve.

Following the loss of Honda engines for 1988, the prospects of the Williams team were poor indeed. Even so, both he and team-mate Riccardo Patrese tried their hardest all season. Nigel regrew his moustache later in the year.

At the Formula 1 testing at Jerez in Spain early in 1988 Nigel Mansell drove a Williams for the first time since his crash in Japan at the beginning of November.

Mansell pits the Judd V8 powered Williams FW11B at the Brazilian Grand Prix. He retired because of overheating problems.

After he had been pushed into the barriers by Alboreto (Ferrari) at the 1988 Monaco Grand Prix.

A Mansell cap for the fans at the 1988 British Grand Prix. Nigel finished second in this wet race behind Senna's McLaren.

Golf is Nigel's other great love and his clubs accompany him to all the races. This photograph was taken at Jerez, scene of the Spanish Grand Prix.

Nigel achieved another second place with the Judd-powered Williams in the 1988 Spanish race after a brilliant drive.

A good enough golfer to take part in the 1988 Australian 'Open', but he failed to make the 'cut'.

Nigel shelters from the intense heat at the 1989 Brazilian Grand Prix.

4 *FERRARI HEARTACHES, 1989-90*

1989

Back in 1986 Mansell had visited Maranello for discussions as to whether he would drive for Ferrari in 1987. They came to nothing, but had been surrounded by some controversy as Ferrari claimed that he had signed a contract, whereas Nigel insisted that the parties had made a written note of their discussions, nothing more. Both parties wanted to forget the past; Ferrari desperately needed a top-line driver alongside Gerhard Berger and the choice was limited, while Nigel needed to break away from Williams hydraulic and electronic unreliability and lack of competitiveness. It was a decision fully backed by Rosanne. Now that he was one of the two fastest drivers in the world and financially independent, thanks to his many business interests, Nigel was able to act as he wanted and his contract with Ferrari was initially for only one year.

The 1989 Ferrari team was very different from that of past years. The team was racing the new 3500cc V12 Tipo 640 car designed by John Barnard and largely developed in Britain at Barnard's GTO establishment (Guildford Technical Office). It was a leaner, fitter organization determined to reassert itself as the dominant team after several years of mediocrity. Although at times Ferrari came close to challenging McLaren supremacy, the Maranello V12 was thoughout the year down on power compared with the V10 Honda used in the McLarens and the cars were plagued by problems with the new and very advanced semi-automatic, electro-hydraulic gearbox.

In the first race of the year Ferrari - and Mansell – scored a remarkable and lucky victory. Senna, with his pole-position McLaren, went off at the first corner after tangling with Berger and following a long pit-stop rejoined the race well down the field. Prost was unable to made a second scheduled pit stop for new tyres because of clutch failure and Nigel scored a comfortable win, almost 8 seconds ahead of the French driver. Next came the San Marino Grand Prix at Imola where Berger's Ferrari crashed because the left front aerofoil had broken - and then burst into flames in front of the world's television audience. Happily Berger's injuries were slight, but the cause of the accident was not esablished until later. Mansell joined the restarted race in worrying ignorance of the cause of his team-mates's crash. Nigel retired because of gearbox trouble and this was the cause of his retirement in the next three races.

The teams moved on to the Canadian Grand Prix at Montreal, where Mansell was disqualified because of the organiser's incompetence. Weather conditions had varied immensely all day and both Nigel and Alessandro Nannini (Benetton) made a late decision to switch from rain tyres to slicks. This meant that both would have to start from the pit lane. When Mansell reached the exit to the pit lane, the exit lights were off and there was no official in charge. Both drivers accelerated cautiously on to the circuit, believing that they were joining the race behind the field. In fact the pack was still on the grid. Mansell and Nannini were disqualified, but Nigel was about to retire in any event because of alternator failure.

More problems followed in France, but by a determined drive Nigel finished second to Prost (McLaren). At the first start Gugelmin (March) had triggered off a multi-car accident and Nigel's Ferrari had been badly damaged. At the restart he took over Berger's intended race car that the Austrian had abandoned because of an oil leak. By the time the oil leak had been repaired, Nigel was obliged to start from the pit lane. Senna retired his McLaren within a few yards of the start and while Prost stroked to an easy and unchallenged win, Mansell was fighting his way through the field, closing to within 44 seconds of the leader by the chequered flag.

Another superb drive followed in the British race where it seemed that Nigel would catch and pass Prost's leading McLaren. His fast run was interupted by a puncture and at the finish he was a little over 19 seconds behind the leader. Outpaced by the McLarens, but trying as hard as ever, Mansell finished third on the fast Hockenheim circuit. In Hungary he tried different tactics and in the second qualifying session he ran his car in race trim, treating practice as though it was part of the race. The result was a place back on the sixth row of the grid, but it was an approach that paid dividends, he carefully preserved his tyres in the opening laps and coming through without a stop for new tyres scored his second win of the season, comfortably ahead of Senna's McLaren. The McLarens dominated the wet Belgian Grand Prix, but in another brilliant drive Nigel pressured Prost for much of the way and took a well deserved third place.

It was now that Nigel's season started to go badly wrong. At Monza he retired again with gearbox problems. Then the Portuguese Grand Prix proved a disaster. The Ferraris had the legs of the McLarens on the Estoril circuit and held first two places for many laps. Mansell was leading when he stopped for new tyres. He overshot the Ferrari pit, and in the confusion of the moment selected reverse gear to manoeuvre the Tipo 640 back to its proper place. It was in clear breach of the regulations. Mansell rejoined the race in fourth place, but soon moved up to third behind team-mate Berger and Senna. The Ferrari pit was told that Mansell had been disqualified and the black flag, accompanied by number 27 was displayed at the start/finish line. Mansell was now challenging Senna for second place and both drivers passed the black flag three times without, apparently, either of them seeing it and without Nigel being warned of his disqualification by radio from the pits. Mansell tried to pass Senna at the first right-hander after the pits, Senna held his line, the two cars collided and both retired with buckled suspension.

When Nigel Mansell left after the Portuguese Grand Prix he had aleady been notified that a US $50,000 fine had been imposed. It was only the following Tuesday that he learned that he had been suspended from the Spanish Grand Prix the next weekend. On the Thursday he held a conference at the Jerez circuit, anxious to assure the world's press that he had not seen the black flag. And he added the threat, 'If they [FISA] believe honestly that I saw [the black flag] and ignored it, I will have to consider retiring sooner rather than later from Formula 1.' Ferrari had appealed against the disqualification, but the appeal could not be heard until after the Spanish race and on 13 October was withdrawn.

The remainder of the season brought Nigel little joy. He retired in Japan because of engine trouble and in the rain-soaked Australian Grand Prix was one of many drivers to slide off. In the World Championship he took fourth place with 38 points.

1990

Nigel signed on for a second season with Ferrari and although the modified Ferrari Tipo 641 cars were more competitive, it was to prove a confused and unhappy year for the

In a season in which the new Ferrari V12 proved unreliable and no real match for the McLarens, Nigel Mansell scored an unexpected, but encouraging victory in the first race of the year in Brazil.

British driver. Alain Prost had joined Ferrari from McLaren and at the Ferrari Press Conference in February Nigel was adamant that he welcomed the French Champion into the team and was happy to work with him; this was a view that soon changed. The charismatic Frenchman soon became the idol of Maranello, the centre of attention and a disheartened Mansell, who craved a one to one working relationship with his team and needed to be the centre of attention became confused and sometimes apathetic. The British driver's spirits were also dampened by a series of mechanical failures. It was a gradual process of erosion of Mansell's spirit that reached its peak in mid-season. Once negotiations for 1991 had reopened with Williams, Nigel's spirit and determination revived and towards the end of the year he again turned in some brilliant drives.

In the first race of the year, the United States Grand Prix at Phoenix the Ferraris proved outclassed and unreliable. Mansell's exit from the race was spectacular, for as he passed the start/finish line flat-out at the end of lap 49 the clutch exploded, the oil tank was punctured, the transmission locked in a flash of fire, oil sprayed over the rear tyres and Nigel spun to rest just before the first corner. Senna failed in Brazil, Prost won for Ferrari and Mansell struggled with faulty roll-bar adjustment to finish fourth. Another retirement because of engine trouble followed at Imola – although at one stage in the race Nigel held second place – and both Ferraris retired at Monaco. Disillusionment was beginning to set in. In Canada Mansell took third place, the first time in 1990 that he appeared on the rostrum at the finish and the delighted smile told everything. It was a brief happy spell, for Prost and Mansell finished fourth and second at Mexico City. Good fortune appeared to be continuing at the Paul Ricard circuit, scene of the French race, where Nigel took a sizzling pole position. At the start Berger jumped Mansell, Senna took second place and although the

Mansell with the Tipo 640 Ferrari did well to finish second to Prost's McLaren in the 1989 French Grand Prix. His race car was badly damaged by Gugelmin's March in a first lap multi-car accident and he had joined the restart from the pit lane with Berger's race car which the Austrian had abandoned because of an oil leak.

With Rosanne and son Leo at the 1989 British Grand Prix.

Nigel's second victory of the season came in the Hungarian Grand Prix. He is leading Nelson Piquet's Lotus 101.

The Ferrari driver was disqualified for reversing in the pit lane at the Portugese Grand Prix. As Mansell and Senna battled for the lead neither saw the black flag. The duel ended as they collided at a high-speed turn. Mansell was suspended from the next race, the Spanish Grand Prix.

At the Spanish Grand Prix Nigel Mansell held a press conference to explain his version of the events at Estoril.

Mansell's name appeared in the entry list at Estoril and the team brought along his race car and spare, hoping that FISA would relax the suspension. They did not and his Ferrari remained firmly under wraps.

The last two races of the year brought Nigel little joy. In Japan (above) he retired because of engine failure and in the Australian Grand Prix (below) he finished against the barriers, like so many other drivers, as the race was held in torrential rain.

Nigel Mansell and his new team-mate Alain Prost at the Ferrari Press Conference at the 1990 United States Grand Prix at Phoenix.

British driver led briefly, he fell back with a sick engine which blew up eight laps from the finish. After the race Nigel commented that it was the worst engine that he had ever had.

Nigel's misery was made all the more by the fact that team-mate Prost came through to win and there was no doubt that the Ferraris could be a serious challenge to McLaren supremacy on some circuits. But to Nigel it was becoming evident that he was receiving second-rate treatment from Maranello and by the next race at Silverstone he had made a momentous, albeit short-lived, decision. Again Mansell took pole position and although Senna led at the start, the Ferraris had by half-race distance settled in first and second places, Mansell leading Prost.

As the race progressed, so Nigel's gear-change became increasingly difficult. Prost took the lead and nine laps from the finish the British driver's Ferrari stopped out on the circuit. By the time Mansell reached the paddock he was raging. To the television cameras he blurted, 'Up to the point where I first experienced gear-change trouble I was much quicker than anybody else. Obviously I'm very happy for Ferrari, but I am bound to wonder why these problems don't seem to happen to the other guy.' Within half-an-hour Mansell announced that he intended to retire at the end of the year, something he said that he had hoped to be able to do on the rostrum if he had won the race.

When Mansell understeered off the track at Hockenheim, caused, he believed, by debris that had collected under his car, he retired in the pits with a damaged front wing. Perhaps, said a cautious Ferrari spokesman, Nigel thought that the car was more badly damaged than it really was. But underneath the surface relations between driver and team were close to breaking point. In Hungary Nigel rose to third place before being forced off the track by Berger, badly wrenching his right wrist. At the start in Belgium Piquet's Benetton shunted Mansell's Ferrari into the pit wall; and in the restarted race Mansell drove apathetically before coming into the pits to retire with handling problems and a vociferous argument with the pit staff. Prost's second place at Spa rubbed more salt into the wound. More problems followed in Italy where Prost finished second, but Nigel fell back because of throttle spring problems and finished an unhappy fourth.

So far it had been a disastrous, almost barren season for the British driver, but there was a change of fortune in Portugal. Probably more than a little associated with his recently started negotiations for 1991 with the Williams team, Nigel took pole position in practice with Prost alongside and, an early mistake apart, drove a superb race. When the light turned green, Mansell turned on too much power, veered across towards Prost who was forced to lift off and the McLarens accelerated cleanly from the second row through the gap and into first two places. Mansell fought his way back to the lead on lap 50 and, despite barging Alliot's Ligier which spun into the barriers, went on to score his first win of the season. Prost finished third. After the race Nigel conceded that 'it must have been the worst start of my life' and although he apologized profusely to the Frenchman, Prost was unappeased.

Next came the Spanish race at Jerez where Mansell finished a strong second to his team-mate. He retired because of a broken drive-shaft in Japan after his stop for new tyres and rounded off the season with another second place at Adelaide. Senna won the Drivers' Championship with 78 points to the 71 of Prost and Mansell trailed a poor fifth with 37 points. By the end of the year Ferrari and Mansell were glad to see the back of each other.

At Monaco in 1990 Nigel Mansell follows Thierry Boutsen (Williams) through Loews Hairpin. Mansell was in fourth place when he was eliminated by electrical problems.

Mansell leads Berger (McLaren) and Prost (Ferrari) in the 1990 British Grand Prix, urged on by his enthusiastic supporters. Mansell retired because of gearbox problems.

Mansell supporters at the British Grand Prix.

Amongst Nigel Mansell's many interests was the Mansell Madgwick Motorsport Formula 3000 team.
Nigel is seen with Madgwick driver, Andrea Montermini, at the 1990 German race.

Nigel and Rosanne at Hockenheim in 1990.

Mansell starts to lose the Ferrari at the second start at the Belgium Grand Prix. He slewed into the barrier and the race was stopped again. After the third start Nigel drove a lacklustre race and retired because of handling problems.

Nigel Mansell prepares for battle.

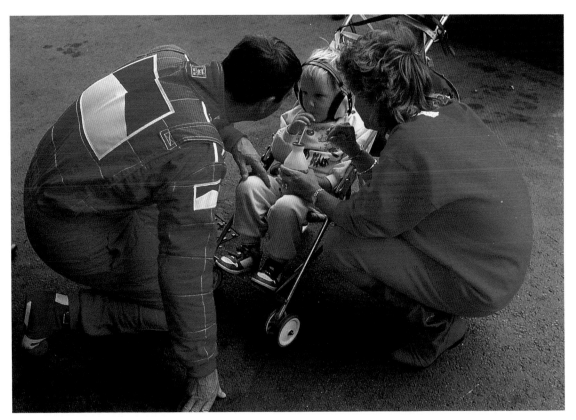

Nigel with Rosanne and younger son, Greg.

After winning the Portugese Grand Prix Nigel embraces Ayrton Senna who finished second. Is that a look of sheer terror on Ayrton's face?

As the season progressed, so the Ferraris improved in speed and reliability. In the Portugese Grand Prix at Estoril Nigel Mansell came through to take the lead and score his first win of the year.

Next came the Spanish race where, the Ferrari drivers took the first two places. Mansell is seen on his way to second place.

Nigel Mansell at the 1990 Spanish Grand Prix.

The 1990 Japanese Grand Prix proves that Nigel Mansell supporters are worldwide.

Although he led the race for many laps, Nigel Mansell retired in the Japanese Grand Prix because of drive-shaft failure.

Australia, 1990. After Mansell had slid down an escape road in his battle with Senna, and Senna had retired, the British Driver finished second behind Piquet (Benetton).

5 RETURN TO DIDCOT:1991

When Nigel Mansell returned to Williams for the 1991 season their relationship had changed substantially. Nigel was now an accepted and recognized 'superstar'. Williams now had substantial backing from Renault, whose turbocharged engines the team had been using since 1989 and the latest RS3 engine was formidable in both power and reliability terms. After three seasons of comparative mediocrity, Williams had been transformed; the team was, technically, vastly improved, the organisation was much tauter and Nigel enjoyed undisputed number one status. Alongside him in the team was Riccardo Patrese, veteran Italian driver, who had been with Williams since 1988 and, remarkably, was to prove quicker than Mansell in qualifying during the first part of the season. The 1991 car was the FW14, with excellent chassis and superb aerodynamics, but plagued by problems with with the team's new semi-automatic gearbox.

McLaren remained the most serious opposition and Senna with the Honda-powered MP4/6 was destined to win the Drivers' Championship again, mainly because the team was able to make such a good start to the season, while Williams struggled to achieve reliability, but also because of Mansell's misfortunes later in the year. The other McLaren driver Gerhard Berger, in his second year with the team, remained overshadowed and demoralized by Senna's brilliance, although he was to win the last race of the year. Benetton remained a strong second force and Piquet won a single race for the team, while Ferrari, where Prost had been joined by the brilliant Franco-Sicilian Jean Alesi, sank into increasing disarray.

The first race of the 1991 season was the United States Grand Prix at Phoenix where Senna took pole position to lead throughout and win from Prost. The Williams FW14s started from the second row of the grid, Patrese slightly faster than Mansell, but although Nigel held third place for almost half the race, both entries were eliminated by gearbox trouble.

Senna repeated this performance at the next round at Interlagos in Brazil, chased by Mansell and Patrese, who had been second fastest in practice; but Mansell again retired with gearbox trouble and Patrese finished second. At Imola Senna again took pole and won, from team-mate Berger, but Patrese had led for the first nine laps. Nigel's race was soon over. At the start he slid left across the road as he struggled with the gearbox and he and Brundle (Brabham) collided.

Then came Monaco. Senna yet again took pole position and led throughout to score his fourth successive win of the year. But Mansell's fortunes were changing. Nigel drove a fine race, holding fourth place for many laps, moving up a place when team-mate Patrese retired, passing Prost for second place in a brilliantly timed move at the chicane and finishing a little over 18 seconds behind Senna at the finish. It was Mansell's best performance ever at Monaco and it was now that he started his furious and fruitless chase of the Championship. In Canada Patrese and Mansell took first two places on the grid and Nigel led until the last lap when the engine cut out a mile before the flag. Victory went to Piquet (Benetton) and a bitterly disappointed Mansell was classified sixth. Both Senna and Berger retired their McLarens.

Patrese and Mansell were again fastest in practice at Mexico City and although Nigel led in the opening laps, his engine was down on power and Patrese went ahead. During the race Mansell was instructed from the pits to richen the mixture and this gave sufficient recovery of power to enable Nigel to counter-attack in the closing laps. But it was not enough and at the finish he was still just over a second behind his Italian team-mate. In 1991 the French Grand Prix was held at Magny-Cours for the first time and Alain Prost with the new and improved 643 Ferrari dominated much of the race. Mansell held second place until he passed Prost on lap 22, slipped back to second again after the routine tyre stops and passed Prost again on lap 55. For the remaining 17 laps Mansell was unchallenged and went on to score his first win of the year, ahead of Prost and Senna. In the World Championship Senna led with 48 points to the 23 of Mansell, but there were still nine races to go ...

On home ground at Silverstone Nigel took pole position and led throughout to the rapture of his supporters. The Williams was now more than a match for the McLaren, but Senna held second place until he ran out of fuel on the last lap and was classified fourth. The gap in the Championship was now down to 18 points, Senna 51, Mansell 33. McLaren's disarray continued in the German race at Hockenheim. Nigel took pole position and led throughout except for a couple of laps after his routine pit stop; Patrese finished second. Senna again ran out of fuel and was classified seventh. The score was now Senna 51 points, Mansell 43 and Nigel seemed to be in with a real chance.

After a poor start to the season Williams - and Nigel Mansell - bounced back at Monaco. In a brilliant move he has just passed Prost going into the chicane and is on his way to second place.

Shortly after this photograph was taken, Prost shot into the pits for a set of new tyres, while Nigel carried on to his best finish at Monaco - he was second again in 1992.

By the Hungarian race McLaren had sorted some of their problems, and the Hungaroring was a circuit better suited to the Honda-powered cars than the Williams. Senna took pole position and led throughout, but Mansell was second, ahead of team-mate Patrese. In Belgium everything went wrong for Nigel. Senna took pole position and he and Mansell battled furiously for the lead: Mansell went ahead after the routine tyre stop, but electrical failure brought him to a halt out on the circuit. Alesi then led with his Ferrari until engine trouble stopped him and Senna went on to win from team-mate Berger. Then came the Italian Grand Prix. Senna led initially, but Nigel pressured him as hard as he dared; Patrese came through to take up the challenge and forced his way through into the lead. When the Italian dropped out because of clutch failure after only one lap in the lead, Nigel resumed the pressure, Senna faltered because of locking brakes and the Williams took a lead that it never lost. In the Championship Senna led with 77 points to the 59 of Mansell, but Nigel was still in with a chance, albeit a slim one.

In Portugal Mansell's Championship hopes were destroyed by a team mistake. Patrese led initially, then Mansell went ahead; at his routine tyre stop Nigel was waved back into the race before the right rear wheel had been secured. As Mansell accelerated away, so the wheel parted company and rolled through the Tyrrell pit. A replacement wheel was attached and Mansell rejoined the race in 17th place. While Nigel battled to make up lost ground, the stewards deliberated and after 16 laps Mansell was disqualified because the car had been worked on away from the inner of the three pit lanes. Williams team manager Peter Windsor accepted full responsibility, but as Nigel commented as he trudged back to the team's motorhome, only too obviously close to tears, 'What more do I have to do?' Patrese won the race with Senna in second place.

Another brilliant win for Nigel followed in Spain and after a spin Senna finished a mediocre fifth. With 69 points to Senna's 85, it was still mathematically possible for Mansell to win the Championship, but not likely. When Mansell spun off in the Japanese Grand Prix, Senna clinched his third World Championship. Berger won with Senna in second place. The final race was the Australian Grand Prix, almost a farce, run in torrential rain and stopped after 14 laps. When the flag fell Senna led and Mansell was in second place. The final Championship score was Senna, 96 points; Mansell, 72 points; Patrese, 53 points. Nigel - and Williams - were determined that 1992 would be very different.

The Williams team showed almost complete domination at Mexico City in 1991. Mansell leads Patrese early in the race, but on lap 15 the Italian went ahead and Nigel had to settle for second place.

Nigel Mansell at the 1991 Mexican Grand Prix.

Riccardo Patrese, Nigel Mansell and third-place driver Ayrton Senna on the podium at Mexico City.
Nigel shows his feelings only too clearly.

Although it was to prove too little, too late, Nigel steadily eroded Senna's lead in the 1991 World Championship. In the French Grand Prix he takes the chequered flag for his first win of the year.

The coy challenger.

A familiar part of the 1991 season was the regular session when the press was given the 'word according to Nige.'

After winning the 1991 British Grand Prix, Nigel gave his rival Ayrton Senna a lift back to the pits. Senna was classified fourth after running out of fuel.

Nigel Mansell salutes the crowd from the podium at Silverstone

Another brilliant victory followed in Germany where Mansell took pole position and, apart from two laps when he made his pit stop for new tyres, led throughout.

During a 'friendly' football match Mansell injured his ankle - but not so badly as his expression suggests - and some of the 'opposition' fared worse.

By the Japanese Grand Prix Nigel had closed within 16 points of Senna (69 to 85) but the British driver's race lasted only nine laps before he spun off into a gravel trap and his faint chance of winning the Championship evaporated.

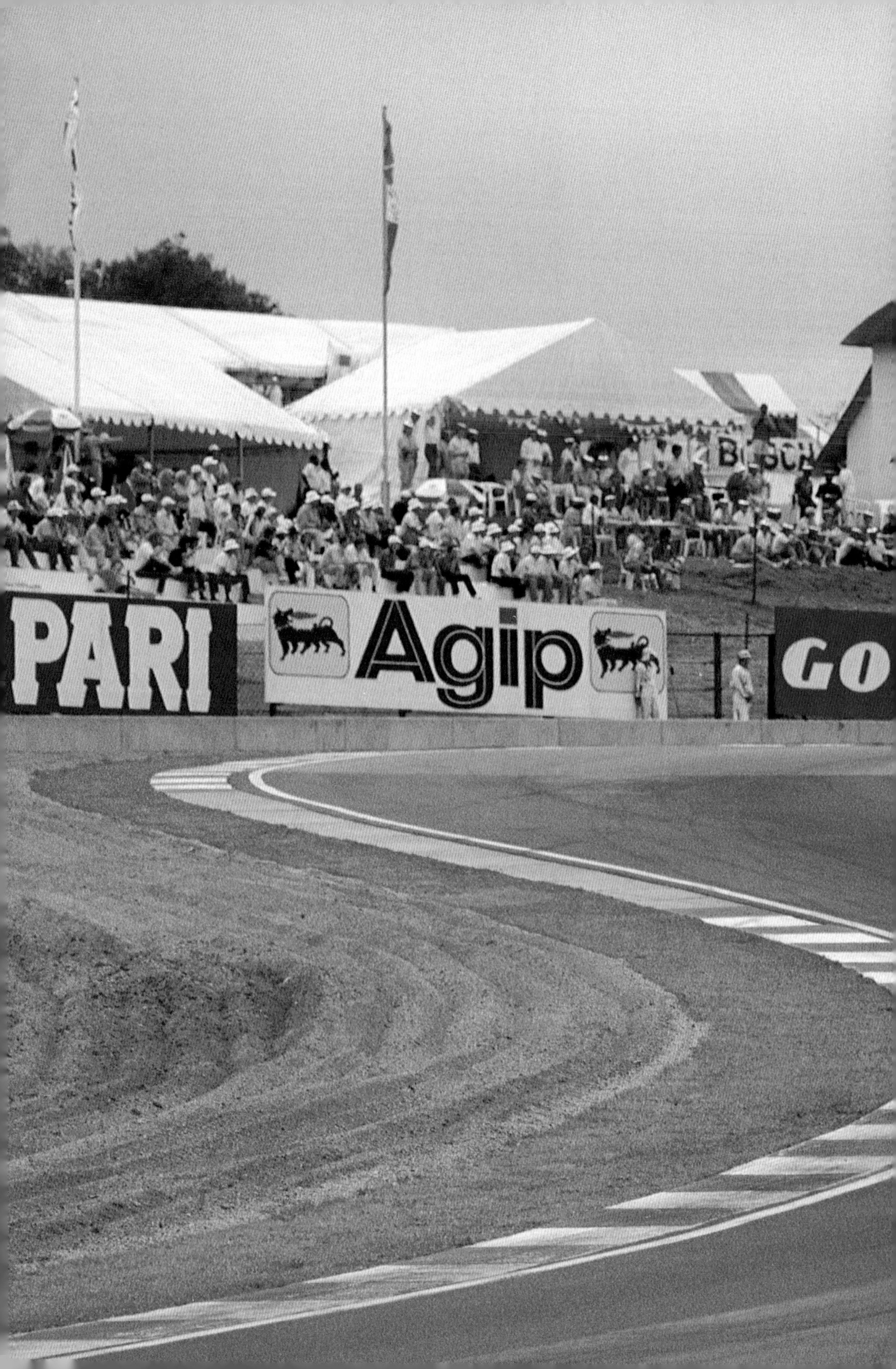
PARI
Agip
GO

The first race of the 1992 season was the South African Grand Prix and such was the supremacy of the Williams that Nigel was able to pull out this lead on the first lap. He and Patrese took the first two places.

6 CHAMPIONSHIP RUN, 1992

Williams entered the 1992 season on a high, with the improved FW14B featuring 'Active' computer-controlled suspension and a much more powerful engine. The driver pairings were the same, Mansell and Patrese. McLaren, at the start of the season, were stuck with the MP4/6B, a slightly modified version of the 1991 car and, as it soon became evident, no match for Didcot. Ferrari had introduced the radical F92A, which proved a dismal failure, and Benetton were best of the rest.

At the first race of the year, the South African Grand Prix, on the much revised Kyalami circuit, Williams demonstrated a marked superiority. Mansell took pole position and at the start of the race he went straight into the lead, with Patrese coming through from the second

The heat and the strain have taken their toll. Mansell on the podium after his victory in South Africa.

row to take station behind his team-mate. As the photograph shows, the Williams team outstripped the opposition from the green light and already on the first lap had pulled out a substantial lead. Nigel and Patrese led throughout, Nigel could hardly have had a more dominant race and at the flag he had a lead of over 24 seconds. After the race Nigel was cautious: 'I don't think we have a great advantage ... Renault and Elf have found us a lot more horsepower over the winter, and the Williams team has done a good, solid job.'

Three weeks later the teams competed on the bumpy Autodromo Hermanos Rodriguez circuit at Mexico City. Again Mansell took pole position, with Patrese second on the grid and again the Williams duo led throughout, with Nigel taking the chequered flag just over 8 seconds ahead of his team-mate and Schumacher finished third for Benetton. But despite this domination Nigel was not entirely convinced of the Williams superiority and after the race commented that both he and Patrese believed that they had a better ride over the circuit's bumps in the 1991 race with conventionally suspended cars than with the 'Active' suspension in 1992.

McLaren was fighting back and at the Brazilian race produced the MP4/7, but it was too new, too underdeveloped to present a serious challenge. Mansell and Patrese were fastest in practice, they took first and second places, a lap ahead of Schumacher's Benetton, and at the flag Nigel led by a margin of 30 seconds. Sadly, for some, the Williams domination was becoming boring and as a Williams spokesman commented, 'I hope the others get better'.

When Nigel won the wet Spanish Grand Prix at Catalunya, he had matched Senna's 1991 record of four successive wins and was beginning to look as though he had the World Championship sewn up. The Williams domination was not quite as complete as in earlier races, for Patrese had spun off on lap 20 and hit a wall and Schumacher, who finished second, had been faster than Patrese in practice. At the San Marino Grand Prix the Williams team seemed to dominate more than ever. Mansell and Patrese were first and second fastest in practice and again they led throughout. With five successive victories Nigel had set a new record in Grand Prix racing and with 50 points gained to the 24 of Patrese, 17 of Schumacher and the 8 of Senna and Berger, his World Championship position was becoming impregnable.

Then came Monaco, apparently destined to provide another demonstration of Mansell and Williams superiority. And so it was until very close to the end, when Nigel made an unscheduled pit stop because of a problem with the left rear tyre and lost the lead to Senna's McLaren. The last laps of the race saw Nigel at his best, driving at the peak of his ability, on the knife-edge of adhesion, as he hurled the Williams in pursuit of his McLaren rival. As Nigel commented after the race, 'Ayrton's car was just too wide', a tribute to the Brazilian's skill at keeping the thrusting Williams at bay. Nigel finished a mere seconds behind the McLaren driver after having slashed 3 seconds off the circuit record.

After another 1-2 by Mansell and Patrese in Mexico, the team travelled to Brazil. Patrese led Mansell until his stop for new tyres, but the British driver then took the lead and the result was another Williams 1-2.

Nigel on his way to his third successive win of the season in Brazil.

Nigel Mansell and Riccardo Patrese at the party organized by Elf (the French petroleum company and one of Williams' main sponsors) at the 1992 Brazilian race.

Mansell and Patrese lead away at the start of the Spanish Grand Prix. Nigel won his fourth race of the year, but Patrese spun off and hit a wall on lap 20.

After a late unscheduled pit stop Mansell lost the lead at Monaco. Nigel fought back, but there was no way that he could pass Senna. Grand Prix racing had come alive again.

Appendix

Nigel Mansell's Grand Prix Record, 1980-92
1980 Racing Number: 43

AUSTRIAN GRAND PRIX, Österreichring,
17 August
Retired, Lotus 81B-Cosworth entered by Team Essex Lotus, engine.

DUTCH GRAND PRIX, Zandvoort,
31 August
Retired, Lotus 81B-Cosworth entered by Team Essex Lotus, spun off because of brake problems.

ITALIAN GRAND PRIX, Monza,
14 September
Did not qualify, Lotus 81-Cosworth entered by Team Essex Lotus.

Drivers' World Championship: No points

1981 Racing Number: 12

SOUTH AFRICAN GRAND PRIX, Kyalami,
7 March (non-Championship race)
10th, Lotus 81-Cosworth entered by Team Essex Lotus.

UNITED STATES GRAND PRIX WEST,
Long Beach, 15 March
Retired, Lotus 81-Cosworth entered by Team Essex Lotus, accident.

BRAZILIAN GRAND PRIX, Rio de Janeiro,
29 March
11th, Lotus 81-Cosworth entered by Team Essex Lotus.

ARGENTINE GRAND PRIX, Buenos Aires,
12 April
Retired, Lotus 81-Cosworth entered by Team Essex Lotus, engine.

BELGIAN GRAND PRIX, Zolder, 17 May
3rd, Lotus 81-Cosworth entered by Team Essex Lotus.

MONACO GRAND PRIX, Monte Carlo,
31 May
Retired, Lotus 87-Cosworth entered by Team Essex Lotus, rear suspension.

SPANISH GRAND PRIX, Jarama, 21 June
6th, Lotus 87-Cosworth entered by John Player Team Lotus.

FRENCH GRAND PRIX, Dijon Prenois,
5 July
7th, Lotus 87-Cosworth entered by John Player Team Lotus.

BRITISH GRAND PRIX, Silverstone, 18 July
Did not qualify, Lotus 87-Cosworth entered by John Player Team Lotus. NOTE: entered with 88B which was disqualified after the first practice session.

GERMAN GRAND PRIX, Hockenheim,
2 August
Retired, Lotus 87-Cosworth entered by John Player Team Lotus, fuel leak.

AUSTRIAN GRAND PRIX, Österreichring,
16 August
Retired Lotus 87-Cosworth entered by John Player Team Lotus, engine.

DUTCH GRAND PRIX, Zandvoort,
30 August
Retired, Lotus 87-Cosworth entered by John Player Team Lotus, electrics.

ITALIAN GRAND PRIX, Monza,
13 September
Retired, Lotus 87-Cosworth entered by John Player Team Lotus, handling problems.

CANADIAN GRAND PRIX, Montreal,
27 September
Retired, Lotus 87-Cosworth entered by John Player Team Lotus, collision with Prost.

CAESAR'S PALACE GRAND PRIX,
Las Vegas, 17 October
4th, Lotus 87-Cosworth entered by John Player Team Lotus.

Drivers' World Championship: 14th, 8 points

1982 Racing Number: 12

SOUTH AFRICAN GRAND PRIX, Kyalami,
23 January
Retired, Lotus 87B-Cosworth entered by John Player Team Lotus, electrics.

BRAZILIAN GRAND PRIX, Rio de Janeiro,
21 March
3rd, Lotus 91-Cosworth entered by John Player Team Lotus.

UNITED STATES GRAND PRIX WEST,
Long Beach, 4 April
7th, Lotus 91-Cosworth entered by John Player Team Lotus.

BELGIAN GRAND PRIX, Zolder, 9 May
Retired, Lotus 91-Cosworth entered by John Player Team Lotus, clutch failure.

MONACO GRAND PRIX, Monte Carlo,
23 May
4th, Lotus 91-Cosworth entered by John Player Team Lotus.

UNITED STATES GRAND PRIX
(DETROIT), Detroit, 6 June
Retired, Lotus 91-Cosworth entered by John Player Team Lotus, engine.

CANADIAN GRAND PRIX, Montreal,
13 June
Retired, Lotus-91 Cosworth entered by John Player Team Lotus, collision with Giacomelli.

BRITISH GRAND PRIX, Brands Hatch,
18 July
Retired, Lotus 91-Cosworth entered by John Player Team Lotus, handling problems.

GERMAN GRAND PRIX, Hockenheim,
8 August
9th, Lotus 91-Cosworth entered by John Player Team Lotus.

AUSTRIAN GRAND PRIX, Österreichring,
15 August
Retired, Lotus 91-Cosworth entered by John Player Team Lotus, engine.

SWISS GRAND PRIX, Dijon-Prenois,
29 August
8th, Lotus 91-Cosworth entered by John Player Team Lotus.

ITALIAN GRAND PRIX, Monza,
12 September
7th, Lotus 91-Cosworth entered by John Player Team Lotus.

CAESAR'S PALACE GRAND PRIX,
Las Vegas, 25 September
Retired, Lotus 91-Cosworth entered by John Player Team Lotus.

Drivers' World Championship: 14th, 7 points.

1983 Racing Number: 12

BRAZILIAN GRAND PRIX, Rio de Janeiro,
13 March
12th, Lotus 92-Cosworth entered by John Player Team Lotus.

UNITED STATES GRAND PRIX WEST,
Long Beach, 27 March
12th, Lotus 92-cosworth entered by John Player Team Lotus.

Race of Champions, Brands Hatch, 10 April
(non-Championship race)
Retired, Lotus 93T-Renault entered by John Player Team Lotus, handling problems.

FRENCH GRAND PRIX, Paul Ricard,
17 April
Retired, Lotus 92-Cosworth entered by John Player Team Lotus, pre-race injury, handling problems.

SAN MARINO GRAND PRIX, Imola, 1 May
Retired, Lotus 92-Cosworth entered by John Player Team Lotus, broken rear wing, spin.

MONACO GRAND PRIX, Monte Carlo,
15 May
Retired, Lotus 92-Cosworth entered by John Player Team Lotus, collision with Alboreto.

BELGIAN GRAND PRIX,
Spa-Francorchamps,
22 May
Retired, Lotus 92-Cosworth entered by John Player Team Lotus, gearbox.

UNITED STATES GRAND PRIX
(DETROIT), Detroit, 5 June
6th, Lotus 92-Cosworth entered by John Player Team Lotus.

CANADIAN GRAND PRIX, Montreal,
12 June
Retired, Lotus 92-Cosworth entered by John Player Team Lotus, tyres, handling.

BRITISH GRAND PRIX, Silverstone, 16 July
4th, Lotus 94T-Renault entered by John Player Team Lotus.

GERMAN GRAND PRIX, Hockenheim,
7 August
Retired, Lotus 97T-Renault entered by John Player Team Lotus, engine.

AUSTRIAN GRAND PRIX, Österreichring,
14 August
5th, Lotus 94T-Renault entered by John Player Team Lotus.

DUTCH GRAND PRIX, Zandvoort,
28 August
Retired, Lotus 94T-Renault entered by John Player Team Lotus, spin.

ITALIAN GRAND PRIX, Monza,
11 September
8th, Lotus 94T-Renault entered by John Player Team Lotus.

EUROPEAN GRAND PRIX, Brands Hatch,
25 September
3rd, Lotus 94T-Renault entered by John Player Team Lotus.

SOUTH AFRICAN GRAND PRIX, Kyalami, 15 October
Not classified, Lotus 94T-Renault entered by John Player Team Lotus, gear linkage and tyre problems.

Drivers' World championship: 12th=, 10 points

1984 Racing Number: 12

BRAZILIAN GRAND PRIX, Rio de Janeiro, 25 March
Retired, Lotus 95T-Renault entered by John Player Team Lotus, accident.

SOUTH AFRICAN GRAND PRIX, Kyalami, 7 April
Retired, Lotus 95T-Renault entered by John Player Team Lotus, collapsed turbocharger inlet duct.

BELGIAN GRAND PRIX, Zolder, 29 April
Retired, Lotus 95T-Renault entered by John Player Team Lotus, clutch.

SAN MARINO GRAND PRIX, Imola, 6 May
Retired, Lotus 95T-Renault entered by John Player Team Lotus, brakes, accident.

FRENCH GRAND PRIX, Dijon-Prenois, 20 May
3rd, Lotus 95T-Renault entered by John Player Team Lotus.

MONACO GRAND PRIX, Monte Carlo, 3 June
Retired, Lotus 95T-Renault entered by John Player Team Lotus, accident whilst leading.

CANADIAN GRAND PRIX, Montreal, 17 June
6th, Lotus 95T-Renault entered by John Player Team Lotus.

UNITED STATES GRAND PRIX (DETROIT), Detroit, 24 June
Retired, Lotus 95T-Renault entered by John Player Team Lotus, gearbox.

UNITED STATES GRAND PRIX (DALLAS), Dallas, 8 July
6th, Lotus 95T-Renault entered by John Player Team Lotus. Not running at the finish, gearbox. **STARTED FROM POLE POSITION**

BRITISH GRAND PRIX, Brands Hatch, 22 July
Retired, Lotus 95T-Renault entered by John Player Team Lotus, gearbox.

GERMAN GRAND PRIX, Hockenheim, 5 August
4th, Lotus 95T-Renault entered by John Player Team Lotus.

AUSTRIAN GRAND PRIX, Österreichring, 19 August
Retired, Lotus 95T-Renault entered by John Player Team Lotus, engine.

DUTCH GRAND PRIX, Zandvoort, 26 August
3rd, Lotus 95T-Renault entered by John Player Team Lotus.

ITALIAN GRAND PRIX, Monza, 9 September
Retired, Lotus 95T-Renault entered by John Player Team Lotus, spin.

EUROPEAN GRAND PRIX, Nürburgring, 7 October
Retired, Lotus 95T-Renault entered by John Player Team Lotus, engine.

PORTUGUESE GRAND PRIX, Estoril, 21 October
Retired, Lotus 95T-Renault entered by John Player Team Lotus, loss of brake fluid, spin.

Drivers' World Championship: 9th=, 13 points

1985 Racing Number: 5

BRAZILIAN GRAND PRIX, Rio de Janeiro, 7 April
Retired, Williams FW10-Honda entered by Canon Williams Honda Team, broken exhaust, accident damage.

PORTUGUESE GRAND PRIX, Estoril, 21 April
5th, Williams FW10-Honda entered by Canon Williams Honda Team.

SAN MARINO GRAND PRIX, Imola, 5 May
5th, Williams FW10-Honda entered by Canon Williams Honda Team.

MONACO GRAND PRIX, Monte Carlo, 19 May
7th, Williams FW10-Honda entered by Canon Williams Honda Team.

CANADIAN GRAND PRIX, Montreal, 16 June
6th, Williams FW10-Honda entered by Canon Williams Honda Team.

UNITED STATES GRAND PRIX (DETROIT), Detroit, 23 June
Retired, Williams FW10-Honda entered by Canon Williams Honda Team, brake trouble, accident.

FRENCH GRAND PRIX, Paul Ricard, 8 July
Did not start, Williams FW10-Honda entered by Canon Williams Honda Team, practice accident.

BRITISH GRAND PRIX, Silverstone, 21 July
Retired, Williams FW10-Honda entered by Canon Williams Honda Team, clutch.

GERMAN GRAND PRIX, Nürburgring, 4 August
6th, Williams FW10-Honda entered by Canon Williams Honda Team.

AUSTRIAN GRAND PRIX, Österreichring, 18 August
Retired, Williams FW10-Honda entered by Canon Williams Honda Team, engine.

DUTCH GRAND PRIX, Zandvoort, 25 August
6th, Williams FW10-Honda entered by Canon Williams Honda Team.

ITALIAN GRAND PRIX, Monza, 8 September
11th, Williams FW10-Honda entered by Canon Williams Honda Team. Not running at the finish, engine.

BELGIAN GRAND PRIX, Spa-Francorchamps, 15 September
2nd, Williams FW10-Honda entered by Canon Williams Honda Team.

EUROPEAN GRAND PRIX, Brands Hatch, 6 October
1st, 126.527 mph, Williams FW10-Honda entered by Canon Williams Honda Team.

SOUTH AFRICAN GRAND PRIX, Kyalami, 19 October
1st, 129.840 mph, Williams FW10-Honda entered by Canon Williams Honda Team. **STARTED FROM POLE POSITION**

AUSTRALIAN GRAND PRIX, Adelaide, 3 November
Retired, Williams FW10-Honda entered by Canon Williams Honda Team, transmission.

Drivers' World Championship: 6th, 31 points.

1986 Racing Number: 5

BRAZILIAN GRAND PRIX, Rio de Janeiro, 23 March
Retired, Williams FW11-Honda entered by Canon Williams Honda Team, accident with Senna.

SPANISH GRAND PRIX, Jerez, 13 April
2nd, Williams FW11-Honda entered by Canon Williams Honda Team.

SAN MARINO GRAND PRIX, Imola, 27 April
Retired, Williams FW11-Honda entered by Canon Williams Honda Team, engine.

MONACO GRAND PRIX, Monte Carlo, 11 May
4th, Williams FW11-Honda entered by Canon Williams Honda Team.

BELGIAN GRAND, PRIX, Spa-Francorchamps, 25 May
1st, 126.479 mph, Williams FW11-Honda entered by Canon Williams Honda Team.

CANADIAN GRAND PRIX, Montreal, 15 June
1st, 110.744 mph, Williams FW11-Honda entered by Canon Williams Honda Team. **STARTED FROM POLE POSITION**

UNITED STATES GRAND PRIX (DETROIT), 22 June
5th, Williams FW11-Honda entered by Canon Williams Honda Team.

FRENCH GRAND PRIX, Paul Ricard, 6 July
1st, 116.856 mph, Williams FW11-Honda entered by Canon Williams Honda Team.

BRITISH GRAND PRIX, Brands Hatch, 13 July
1st, 129.775 mph, Williams FW11-Honda entered by Canon Williams Honda Team.

GERMAN GRAND PRIX, Hockenheim, 27 July
3rd, Williams FW11-Honda entered by Canon Williams Honda Team.

HUNGARIAN GRAND PRIX, Hungaroring, 10 August
3rd, Williams FW11-Honda entered by Canon Williams Honda Team.

AUSTRIAN GRAND PRIX, Österreichring, 17 August
Retired, Williams FW11-Honda entered by Canon Williams Honda Team, drive-shaft failure.

ITALIAN GRAND PRIX, Monza,
7 September
2nd, Williams FW11-Honda entered by Canon
Williams Honda Team.

PORTUGUESE GRAND PRIX, Estoril,
21 September
1st, 116.596 mph, Williams FW11-Honda entered
by Canon Williams Honda Team.

MEXICAN GRAND PRIX, Mexico City,
12 October
5th, Williams FW11-Honda entered by Canon
Williams Honda Team.

AUSTRALIAN GRAND PRIX, Adelaide,
26 October
Retired, Williams FW11-Honda entered by Canon
Williams Honda Team, tyre failure, accident.
STARTED FROM POLE POSITION

Drivers ' World Championship: 2nd, 72 points

1987 Racing Number: 5

BRAZILIAN GRAND PRIX, Rio de Janeiro,
12 April
6th, Williams F11B-Honda entered by Canon
Williams Honda Team. **STARTED FROM
POLE POSITION**

SAN MARINO GRAND PRIX, Imola, 3 May
1st, 121.292 mph , Williams F11 B-Honda entered
by Canon Williams Team Honda.

BELGIAN GRAND PRIX,
Spa-Francorchamps,
17 May
Retired, Williams FW11B-Honda entered by
Canon Williams Honda Team, accident damage
following collision with Senna. **STARTED
FROM POLE POSITION**

MONACO GRAND PRIX, Monte Carlo,
31 May
Retired, Williams FW11B-Honda entered by
Canon Williams Honda Team, turbocharger
wastegate pipe failure. **STARTED FROM POLE
POSITION**

**UNITED STATES (DETROIT) GRAND
PRIX, 21 June**
5th, Williams FW11B-Honda entered by Canon
Williams Honda Team. **STARTED FROM
POLE POSITION**

FRENCH GRAND PRIX, Paul Ricard,
5 July
1st, 117.165 mph , Williams FW11 B-Honda
entered by Canon Williams Honda Team.
STARTED FROM POLE POSITION

BRITISH GRAND PRIX, Silverstone, 12 July
1st, 146.208 mph, Williams FW11B-Honda entered
by Canon Williams Honda Team.

GERMAN GRAND PRIX, Hockenheim,
26 July
Retired, Williams FW11B-Honda entered by
Canon Williams Honda Team, engine. **STARTED
FROM POLE POSITION**

HUNGARIAN GRAND PRIX, Hungaroring,
9 August
14th, Williams FW11B-Honda entered by Canon
Williams Honda Team. Not running at the finish,
lost wheel nut. **STARTED FROM POLE
POSITION**

AUSTRIAN GRAND PRIX, Österreichring,
16 August
1st, 146.283 mph, Williams FW11B-Honda entered
by Canon Williams Honda Team.

ITALIAN GRAND PRIX, Monza,
6 September
3rd, Williams FW11B-Honda entered by Canon
Williams Honda Team.

PORTUGUESE GRAND PRIX, Estoril,
21 September
Retired, Williams FW11B-Honda entered by
Canon Williams Honda Team, electrics.

SPANISH GRAND PRIX, Jerez,
27 September
1st, 103.674 mph, Williams FW11B-Honda entered
by Canon Williams Honda Team.

MEXICAN GRAND PRIX, Mexico City,
18 October
1st, 120.189 mph, Williams FW11B-Honda entered
by Canon Williams Honda Team. **STARTED
FROM POLE POSITION**

JAPANESE GRAND PRIX, Suzuka,
1 November
Did not start, Williams FW11B-Honda entered by
Canon Williams Honda Team, practice accident.
NOTE: Riccardo Patrese substituted for Mansell,
still suffering from injuries, in the Australian Grand
Prix.

Drivers' World Championship: 2nd, 61 points

1988 Racing Number: 5

BRAZILIAN GRAND PRIX, Rio de Janeiro,
3 April
Retired, Williams FW12-Judd entered by Canon
Williams Team, overheating.

SAN MARINO GRAND PRIX, Imola, 1 May
Retired, Williams FW12-Judd entered by Canon
Williams Team, engine, electrics.

MONACO GRAND PRIX, Monte Carlo,
15 May
Retired, Williams FW12-Judd entered by Canon
Williams Team, collision with Alboreto.

MEXICAN GRAND PRIX, Mexico City,
29 May
Retired, Williams FW12-Judd entered by Canon
Williams Team, engine.

CANADIAN GRAND PRIX, Montreal,
12 June
Retired, Williams FW12-Judd entered by Canon
Williams Team, engine.

**UNITED STATES GRAND PRIX
(DETROIT), Detroit, 19 June**
Retired, Williams FW12-Judd entered by Canon
Williams Team, electrics.

FRENCH GRAND PRIX, Paul Ricard, 3 July
Retired, Williams FW12-Judd entered by Canon
Williams Team, suspension.

BRITISH GRAND PRIX, Silverstone, 10 July
2nd, Williams FW12-Judd entered by Canon Williams
Team.

GERMAN GRAND PRIX, Hockenheim,
24 July
Retired, Williams FW12-Judd entered by Canon
Williams Team spin.

HUNGARIAN GRAND PRIX, Hungaroring,
7 August
Retired, Williams FW12-Judd entered by Canon
Williams Team, driver exhaustion.
NOTE: Mansell missed the Belgian and Italian
Grand Prix because of illness.

PORTUGUESE GRAND PRIX, Estoril,
25 September
Retired, Williams FW12-Judd entered by Canon
Williams Team, spin.

SPANISH GRAND PRIX, Jerez, 2 October
2nd, Williams FW12-Judd entered by Canon
Williams Team.

JAPANESE GRAND PRIX, Suzuka,
30 October
Retired, Williams FW12-Judd entered by Canon
Williams Team, spin.

AUSTRALIAN GRAND PRIX, Adelaide,
13 November
Retired, Williams FW12-Judd entered by Canon
Williams Team, brake problems, spin.

Drivers World Championship: 10th, 12 points

1989 Racing Number: 27

BRAZILIAN GRAND PRIX, Rio de Janeiro,
26 March
1st, 115.595 mph, Ferrari Tipo 640 entered by
Scuderia Ferrari SpA.

SAN MARINO GRAND PRIX, Imola,
23 April
Retired, Ferrari Tipo 640 entered by Scuderia
Ferrari SpA, gearbox.

**MONTE CARLO GRAND PRIX, Monte
Carlo,**
7 May
Retired, Ferrari Tipo 640 entered by Scuderia
Ferrari SpA, gearbox.

MEXICAN GRAND PRIX, Mexico City,
28 May
Retired, Ferrari Tipo 640 entered by Scuderia
Ferrari SpA, gearbox.

UNITED STATES GRAND PRIX, Phoenix,
4 June
Retired, Ferrari Tipo 640 entered by Scuderia
Ferrari SpA, gearbox.

CANADIAN GRAND PRIX, Montreal,
18 June
Disqualified, Ferrari Tipo 640 entered by Scuderia
Ferrari SpA. Did not follow correct start procedure.

FRENCH GRAND PRIX, Paul Ricard, 9 July
2nd, Ferrari Tipo 640 entered by Scuderia Ferrari
SpA.

BRITISH GRAND PRIX, Silverstone,
16 July
2nd, Ferrari Tipo 640 entered by Scuderia Ferrari
SpA.

GERMAN GRAND PRIX, Hockenheim,
30 July
3rd, Ferrari Tipo 640 entered by Scuderia Ferrari
SpA.

HUNGARIAN GRAND PRIX, Hungaroring,
13 August
1st, 103.821 mph, Ferrari Tipo 640 entered by
Scuderia Ferrari SpA.

BELGIAN GRAND PRIX,
Spa-Francorchamps, 27 August
3rd, Ferrari Tipo 640 entered by Scuderia Ferrari SpA.

ITALIAN GRAND PRIX, Monza,
10 September
Retired, Ferrari Tipo 640 entered by Scuderia Ferrari SpA, gearbox.

PORTUGUESE GRAND PRIX, Estoril,
24 September
Disqualified, Ferrari Tipo 640 entered by Scuderia Ferrari SpA, reversing in the pit lane (stopped by collision with Senna).

SPANISH GRAND PRIX, Jerez, 1 October
Entered, but suspended from this race following the disqualification at Estoril.

JAPANESE GRAND PRIX, Suzuka,
22 October
Retired, Ferrari Tipo 640 entered by Scuderia Ferrari SpA, engine.

AUSTRALIAN GRAND PRIX, Adelaide,
5 November
Retired, Ferrari Tipo 640 entered by Scuderia Ferrari SpA, spin.

Drivers' World Championship: 4th, 38 points

1990 Racing Number: 2

UNITED STATES GRAND PRIX, Phoenix,
11 March
Retired, Ferrari Tipo 641 entered by Scuderia Ferrari SpA engine, clutch.

BRAZILIAN GRAND PRIX, Interlagos,
25 March
4th, Ferrari Tipo 641 entered by Scuderia Ferrari SpA.

SAN MARINO GRAND PRIX, Imola,
13 May
Retired, Ferrari Tipo 641 entered by Scuderia Ferrari SpA, engine.

MONACO GRAND PRIX, Monte Carlo,
27 May
Retired, Ferrari Tipo 641 entered by Scuderia Ferrari SpA, electronics.

CANADIAN GRAND PRIX, Montreal,
10 June
3rd, Ferrari Tipo 641 entered by Scuderia Ferrari SpA.

MEXICAN GRAND PRIX, Mexico City,
24 June
2nd, Ferrari Tipo 641 entered by Scuderia Ferrari SpA.

FRENCH GRAND PRIX, Paul Ricard, 8 July
Retired, Ferrari Tipo 641 entered by Scuderia Ferrari SpA, engine.

BRITISH GRAND PRIX, Silverstone, 15 July
Retired, Ferrari Tipo 641 entered by Scuderia Ferrari SpA, gearbox.

GERMAN GRAND PRIX, Hockenheim,
29 July
Retired, Ferrari Tipo 641 entered by Scuderia Ferrari SpA, slid off, nose wing damage.

HUNGARIAN GRAND PRIX, Hungaroring,
12 August
17th, Ferrari Tipo 641 entered by Scuderia Ferrari SpA, not running at the finish, collision with Berger.

BELGIAN GRAND PRIX,
Spa-Francorchamps, 25 August
Retired, Ferrari Tipo 641 entered by Scuderia Ferrari SpA, handling problems.

ITALIAN GRAND PRIX, Monza,
9 September
4th, Ferrari Tipo 641 entered by Scuderia Ferrari SpA.

PORTUGUESE GRAND PRIX, Estoril,
23 September
1st, 120.374 mph, Ferrari Tipo 641 entered by Ferrari SpA.

SPANISH GRAND PRIX, Jerez,
30 September
2nd, Ferrari Tipo 641 entered by Scuderia Ferrari SpA.

JAPANESE GRAND PRIX, Suzuka,
21 October
Retired, Ferrari Tipo 641 entered by Scuderia Ferrari SpA, drive-shaft failure.

AUSTRALIAN GRAND PRIX, Adelaide,
4 November
2nd, Ferrari Tipo 641 entered by Scuderia Ferrari SpA.

Drivers' World Championship: 5th, 37 points

1991 Racing Number: 5

UNITED STATES GRAND PRIX, Phoenix,
10 March
Retired, Williams FW14-Renault entered by Canon Williams Team, gearbox.

BRAZILIAN GRAND PRIX, Interlagos,
24 March
Retired, Williams FW14-Renault entered by Canon Williams Team, gearbox.

SAN MARINO GRAND PRIX, Imola,
28 April
Retired, Williams FW14-Renault entered by Canon Williams Team, collision with Brundle.

MONACO GRAND PRIX, Monte Carlo,
12 May
2nd, Williams FW14-Renault entered by Canon Williams Team.

CANADIAN GRAND PRIX, Montreal,
2 June
6th, Williams FW14-Renault entered by Canon Williams Team, not running at the finish, engine cut out.

MEXICAN GRAND PRIX, Mexico City,
16 June
2nd, Williams FW14-Renault entered by Canon Williams Team.

FRENCH GRAND PRIX, Magny-Cours,
7 July
1st, 116.985 mph, Williams FW14-Renault entered by Canon Williams Team.

BRITISH GRAND PRIX, Silverstone, 14 July
1st, 131.227 mph, Williams FW14-Renault entered by Canon Williams Team. **STARTED FROM POLE POSITION**

GERMAN GRAND PRIX, Hockenheim,
28 July
1st, 143.554 mph, Williams FW14-Renault entered by Canon Williams Team. **STARTED FROM POLE POSITION**

HUNGARIAN GRAND PRIX, Hungaroring,
11 August
2nd, Williams FW14-Renault entered by Canon Williams Team.

BELGIAN GRAND PRIX,
Spa-Francorchamps, 25 August
Retired, Williams FW14-Renault entered Canon Williams Team, voltage regulator.

ITALIAN GRAND PRIX, Monza,
8 September
1st, 147.109 mph, Williams FW14-Renault entered by Canon Williams Team.

PORTUGUESE GRAND PRIX, Estoril,
22 September
Disqualified, Williams FW14-Renault entered by Canon Williams Team, car worked on away from inner pit line.

SPANISH GRAND PRIX, Jerez,
29 September
1st, 116.561 mph, Williams FW14-Renault entered by Canon Williams Team.

JAPANESE GRAND PRIX, Suzuka,
20 October
Retired, Williams FW14-Renault entered by Canon Williams Team, spin.

AUSTRALIAN GRAND PRIX, Adelaide,
3 November
2nd, Williams FW14-Renault entered by Canon Williams Team.

Drivers' World Championship: 2nd, 72 points

1992 Racing Number: 5

SOUTH AFRICAN GRAND PRIX, Kyalami,
1 March
1st, 118.900 mph, Williams FW14B-Renault entered by Canon Williams Team. **STARTED FROM POLE POSITION**

MEXICAN GRAND PRIX, Mexico City,
22 March
1st, 123.762 mph , Williams FW14B-Renault entered by Canon Williams Team. **STARTED FROM POLE POSITION**

BRAZILIAN GRAND PRIX, Interlagos,
5 April
1st, 118.191 mph, Williams FW14B-Renault entered by Canon Williams Team. **STARTED FROM POLE POSITION**

SPANISH GRAND PRIX Catalunya 3 May
1st, 99.017 mph , Williams FW14B-Renault entered by Canon Williams Team. **STARTED FROM POLE POSITION**

SAN MARINO GRAND PRIX, Imola,
17 May
1st, 127.130 mph, Williams FW14B-Renault entered by Canon Williams Team. **STARTED FROM POLE POSITION**

MONACO GRAND PRIX, Monte Carlo,
31 May
2nd, Williams FW14B-Renault entered by Canon Williams Team. **STARTED FROM POLE POSITION**